TREETOPS

20,000 Leagues Under the Sea

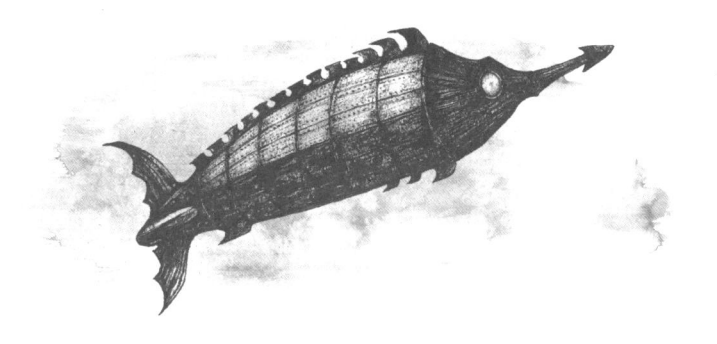

WRITTEN BY JULES VERNE

Adapted by David Tomlinson
Illustrated by David Lupton

OXFORD
UNIVERSITY PRESS

OXFORD
UNIVERSITY PRESS

is a department of the University of Oxford.
It furthers the University's objective of excellence in research, scholarship,
and education by publishing worldwide in

Oxford   New York
Auckland   Cape Town   Dar es Salaam   Hong Kong   Karachi
Kuala Lumpur   Madrid   Melbourne   Mexico City   Nairobi
New Delhi   Shanghai   Taipei   Toronto

With offices in

Argentina   Austria   Brazil   Chile   Czech Republic   France   Greece
Guatemala   Hungary   Italy   Japan   Poland   Portugal   Singapore
South Korea   Switzerland   Thailand   Turkey   Ukraine   Vietnam

Oxford is a registered trade mark of Oxford University Press
in the UK and in certain other countries

Text © David Tomlinson 2008

The moral rights of the author have been asserted

Database right Oxford University Press (maker)

First published 2008

All rights reserved. No part of this publication may be reproduced,
stored in a retrieval system, or transmitted, in any form or by any means,
without the prior permission in writing of Oxford University Press,
or as expressly permitted by law, or under terms agreed with the appropriate
reprographics rights organization. Enquiries concerning reproduction
outside the scope of the above should be sent to the Rights Department,
Oxford University Press, at the address above

You must not circulate this book in any other binding or cover
and you must impose this same condition on any acquirer

British Library Cataloguing in Publication Data

Data available

ISBN: 978-0-19-911769-7

10 9 8 7 6

Cover illustration by Laszlo Veres

Inside illustrations by David Lupton

Printed in Malaysia by
MunSang Printers Sdn Bhd

Paper used in the production of this book is a natural, recyclable product
made from wood grown in sustainable forests. The manufacturing process
conforms to the environmental regulations of the country of origin.

Contents

PART 1
Chapter 1: Sea monster — 5
Chapter 2: Defenceless — 10

PART 2
Chapter 3: The fish of steel — 19
Chapter 4: Blood in the water — 29
Chapter 5: Birds of paradise — 36
Chapter 6: Shark attack — 47
Chapter 7: Trapped — 57
Chapter 8: Freak of nature — 66
Chapter 9: Last battle — 73

PART 3
Chapter 10: Maelstrom — 81
Chapter 11: Final words — 88

PART 1

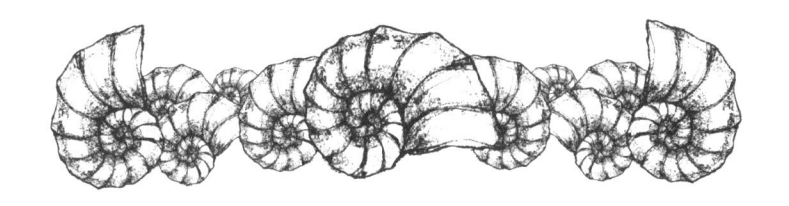

CHAPTER I

Sea monster

The year of 1867 was the year of the sea monster.

A huge creature that glowed in the water appeared from nowhere and rammed several ships at sea. Then it disappeared faster than a killer whale.

Everyone was talking about it. What was it? Did it come from the bottom of the oceans? Or from Outer Space? Whatever it was, people were scared. They wanted the creature hunted down and the seas made safe.

My name is Pierre Aronnax, Professor of Natural History at the Museum of Paris. I was in New York when the sea monster was first spotted. I was there to talk about my new book.

I don't want to be boastful, but it was the most up-to-date book about life under the waves. And because I was an expert on sea life, the *New York Herald* asked me what I thought the sea creature could be.

I said it had to be an unknown sea creature of great size and power that came up from the unexplored depths.

The United States planned an expedition to get rid of the monster, and the *Abraham Lincoln* (the fastest ship in the US navy) was chosen for the job. I was asked to join the trip, together with my friend and assistant, Conseil.

Conseil was worried about the fossils* we had brought to show everyone in New York. 'What will happen to them?' he said.

'They'll be fine. Everything will be sent back to France,' I said. 'I can't turn down the chance of being the first scientist to see this monster. It will be a fantastic mission – even if it is going to be dangerous.'

The idea of danger made Conseil go pale. 'Perhaps I should stay behind with the fossils,' he said. 'I'm much better at making notes on dead creatures than chasing live ones that bite.'

Conseil loved paperwork much more than working outdoors. So I dug the fossils up while he stayed safely at a desk, writing down what I had found. But Conseil did not stay behind. He was a good friend and much too loyal to let me face danger alone.

The captain of the *Abraham Lincoln* was a man called Farragut. He was an experienced and brave seaman, and no ship could have been better armed. We had harpoons* and a gun that fired explosive shot. There was also a cannon that could fire up to ten miles.

But better than all our weapons, we had the famous Ned Land on board. Ned Land was a Canadian harpooner with a sharp eye and a quick arm. He was the best whale hunter alive – tall, strong and cool.

Ned was also the only person on the ship who did not believe in the sea monster.

'Why don't you believe that we're looking for

some kind of a giant whale?' I asked him.

Ned grinned broadly at me. 'A whale couldn't scratch the steel plates of a steamer never mind sink it,' he said.

'But there are stories of ships that have had bites taken out of them by sea creatures,' I said.

'*Wooden* ships, maybe,' replied Ned. 'But ships made of steel? I doubt it. And I'd want to see proof before I'd believe it.'

Weeks passed and nothing happened. We went up and down the North Pacific for two months, but we saw nothing except calm, empty waters. Everybody on the ship became short-tempered and bored. We were beginning to look like fools. Where was this famous sea creature?

'This is stupid,' Conseil said. 'We're wasting our time. This isn't serious scientific work. Everyone is laughing at us.'

'You're right, Conseil,' I admitted. 'We should have gone back to Paris.' But at that moment I heard a voice shouting out through the salt air. It was Ned Land.

'Ahoy!' he cried. 'Look out there! It's the sea monster!'

CHAPTER 2

Defenceless

The whole of the ship's crew raced towards Ned.

My heart beat loudly. A spot in the sea had a spooky glow. Were we about to uncover the mystery of the monster?

'Could it be algae?'* asked Conseil. He was clearly hoping it wasn't a monster.

'No,' I said. 'That light isn't algae. It has to be some sort of electrical power. And look! It's moving.'

'Aye, and straight for us,' said Ned.

The glowing patch of water whizzed towards the *Abraham Lincoln* at the speed of a rocket. The water around it splashed and bubbled. At the last minute it dived below the waves and came up on the other side of our ship.

Captain Farragut was amazed.

'Professor Aronnax,' he said. 'What sort of creature is this? How can we catch it?'

I stared at the gigantic creature. It was unlike anything I'd seen before and I had no idea how to fight it.

The tail of the creature beat violently, frothing up the water as it moved.

I guessed it was at least eighty metres long. As I watched, two jets of steam and water squirted upwards, at least fifty metres into the air. I guessed they were the breathing holes of a whale.

'Put on all steam,' Captain Farragut said grimly.

The time for battle had arrived. The *Abraham Lincoln* steamed straight at the creature at top speed, but to our surprise, we didn't get any closer.

'Put on more steam if you can, sir,' Ned said. 'If we can get closer, I'll harpoon it.'

'Engineer, put on more steam,' Captain Farragut ordered.

Ned got ready to strike. The fires in the engine room of the *Abraham Lincoln* burned red hot. The masts trembled and the narrow funnels choked with smoke. For a whole hour we chased the monster but we could not get any closer. The sailors swore and Captain Farragut chewed on his beard.

Several times we thought it slowed a little, but just as Ned got ready to strike, it swerved away again.

'It's playing with us,' Ned said. 'I just can't get close enough to hit it.'

'Very well,' Captain Farragut said. 'We shall see if it can outrun our cannon.'

The cannon was loaded and fired. The first shot passed harmlessly over the top of the creature.

'To the right!' the captain cried. The next missile seemed to score a direct hit but had no effect at all.

The captain would not give up. 'I'm going to chase that monster until this ship falls apart,' he declared.

Just then I heard a swishing noise and saw Ned's arm whip forward. He had thrown his harpoon at the creature. There was a dull, metallic clang as it struck. Then the light went out on the creature and two enormous waterspouts* broke over the bridge of our ship. Water rushed from one end of the deck to the other, knocking men off their feet. A thundering shock followed, and the ship rocked.

I was taken by surprise and felt myself falling forward. I grabbed helplessly at the rail – and then I tumbled over the side and into the sea.

I rose to the surface, gasping for air, only to see the *Abraham Lincoln* steaming away from me at full speed.

'Help! Help!' I screamed. My waterlogged clothes were dragging me down. I was sinking. But then I felt my arm grabbed by a strong hand, and I was pulled back to the surface. It was Conseil.

'Conseil,' I spluttered. 'Did you fall overboard as well?'

'No, I jumped,' he said.

'You jumped?'

'I needed a bath,' he said.

Conseil had risked his life to save me, but he still found time to joke.

'Why didn't the ship stop to rescue us?' I asked.

'It couldn't. The monster's teeth smashed our rudder,'* Conseil said. 'The ship was out of control.'

We said no more because staying afloat in the choppy sea took all our breath away. As we swam, we took it in turns to pull each other along, so that we could also take it in turns to rest.

It was not long before my strength ran out and I couldn't hold onto Conseil any more. He had to swim for both of us.

'You must leave me,' I said. 'Save yourself.'

But Conseil would not let me go.

A moment later my hand hit something below the surface of the water. I clung to it and felt another helping hand on my arm.

'Ned!' I cried.

'Hold on, and put your feet down,' he told me.

I did as he said, and my feet came to rest on a firm platform. I laughed with relief.

'Did you fall overboard, or jump like Conseil?' I asked.

'I fell,' Ned said. 'But I was luckier than you. I landed on this floating island. Or should I say, onto our mysterious sea monster.'

'The sea monster!' I cried. I couldn't believe what Ned was saying. 'Are we really standing on the creature we've been chasing?'

'Yes,' Ned said. 'And it's made of steel plate. That's why my harpoon bounced off it.'

I kicked the hull* and it rang out like a bell.

16

The monster that had terrified the world wasn't a live creature at all. We were standing on the back of a huge, steel submarine ship! How could that be? Had somebody really built a ship that could sail *underwater?*

I had only just taken this in, when the steel fish began to slip below the surface. It was diving.

All of us scrambled about, searching for an opening in the submarine, but we couldn't find one.

The water rose around our chests and for the second time in a couple of hours it looked as if we were about to drown.

Ned kicked out at the steel plates and yelled, 'Let us in, you monsters!'

The submarine stopped sinking as if it had heard him.

There was a clanking sound and a metal plate lifted. The masked head of a man came into view. Several more masked men followed him, and arms reached out to grab us. Then they dragged us through the manhole* and into the belly of the mysterious submarine.

PART 2

CHAPTER 3

The fish of steel

We were pulled down a metal ladder, and before we had time to look around we were shoved along a corridor and into a prison cell. Two men followed us in.

One of them had a broad back and big muscles. The other one was taller with cold, staring eyes. He looked like the one in charge.

I explained to them who we were. I spoke in French but they didn't reply. I tried speaking in English, German and Italian, but they still didn't answer me.

'Perhaps actions speak louder than words,' Ned said, and before I could stop him he threw the broad-shouldered man to the floor and pinned him down.

'Careful, gentlemen,' the tall man said. He spoke in French so he had understood me after all. 'Don't make me angry. I know who you are. We aren't on land now and I don't have to live by your laws.'

He was deadly serious. Nobody else had a submarine like his. He was all-powerful on the sea – safe to do whatever he wanted, and nobody could stop him.

'Professor Aronnax,' he said. 'You're in my world now, and here you will stay until you die.'

'What?' Ned cried, ready to hit him. 'You mean we'll never see our friends and families again?'

'You are prisoners of war,'* the tall man said. 'You're lucky I didn't let you drown. And now that you know the secret of my submarine, I cannot let you go.'

Ned raised a fist but I held him back. Even if we could fight our way out of the cell, how would we escape the submarine without drowning?

'Who are you?' I asked the tall man.

'My name is Captain Nemo,' he said. 'And you are aboard the *Nautilus*, the most powerful ship in all the oceans.'

It was hard to believe that we were really prisoners. Before taking us to our cabins, Captain Nemo showed us round the ship. I could only think that he wanted to show it off.

First, we went into a huge room that Nemo called the saloon. The walls were covered with shelves full of hundreds of books.

'Amongst these books you will find yours, Professor – *Mysteries of the Underwater World*,' Nemo said calmly.

I was strangely pleased to think that he had already heard of me.

'But that book is just the beginning,' Nemo said. 'You will learn a lot more about the underwater world on board the *Nautilus*.'

Apart from books, there were many other treasures in the saloon. It was like being in a museum full of things that lived in the sea or were lost at sea. There were glass cases of fossils and shells, and aquariums full of coral, seaweed, and multi-coloured fish. There were broken stone pillars from the lost city of Atlantis,* bronze fittings from the Greek ships that attacked Troy, Viking helmets, pieces of Roman armour, and a dagger that had belonged to Christopher Columbus.

This was the greatest kind of treasure for a scientist and a historian like myself. I could write another book on the study of these finds alone.

But Ned was not interested in treasure like this. His eyes were on the chests of gold coins, rescued from sunken Spanish galleons,* and the piles of rubies and diamonds wrapped in a skull and crossbones pirate flag, brought up from the seabed of the Caribbean.

Against one wall there was a large piano. Nemo played a few dramatic chords on it as we looked around.

There was more science, history and wealth in this one room than in all the museums and banks of Europe put together.

'I can tell you like the sea, Captain,' Conseil said, half joking.

'The sea is everything to me,' Nemo said seriously. 'It's a pure and clean place. The sea does not belong to evil rulers. Here I am free.'

A few moments later, we passed an iron ladder. Ned asked what it was for.

'It leads to a small boat on the upper part of the *Nautilus*,' Nemo said. 'There's a manhole from the *Nautilus* to an airtight compartment in the small boat. When the small boat is set loose, the airtight compartment lets us breathe until we get to the surface.'

'Worth remembering,' Ned whispered to me under his breath. 'For when we make our escape.'

I said nothing. After seeing the library of books and the treasures, I couldn't think of escape. I could only think of getting to look at them again.

Nemo was showing us the engine room. 'My new technology gives my engines endless power,' he explained. 'You saw the jets of water from my pumps that burst over the *Abraham Lincoln*.'

'Of course,' I said. 'We thought they were the blowholes* of a whale.'

'But how did you build the *Nautilus* without anybody knowing?' Conseil asked.

'Each section was made in a different part of the world. They were then sent to a secret workshop where they were all put together,' Nemo said.

We returned to the saloon and Nemo left us alone to get used to our new home.

'Well,' Ned said. 'Any ideas about how we are going to escape?'

'I want to forget escaping for the time being,' I answered.

'Forget about escaping?' Ned said. 'Are you mad?'

'This is my great chance,' I said. 'I could write the best book of my life on this ship.'

'Isn't your freedom worth more than a book?' Ned asked.

'The professor is giving up his freedom for the greater good of science,' Conseil said, in my defence.

'Don't you understand, Ned,' I said. 'I've *got* to see more of this underwater world. I need to learn about it.'

'See?' Ned scoffed. 'But we can't see anything in this steel box...'

A sliding noise interrupted him. Light burst into the saloon. Part of the wall opened to show a window that looked out under the surface of the sea. The water was lit up for a mile in all directions.

Sea creatures of all kinds swam before me.

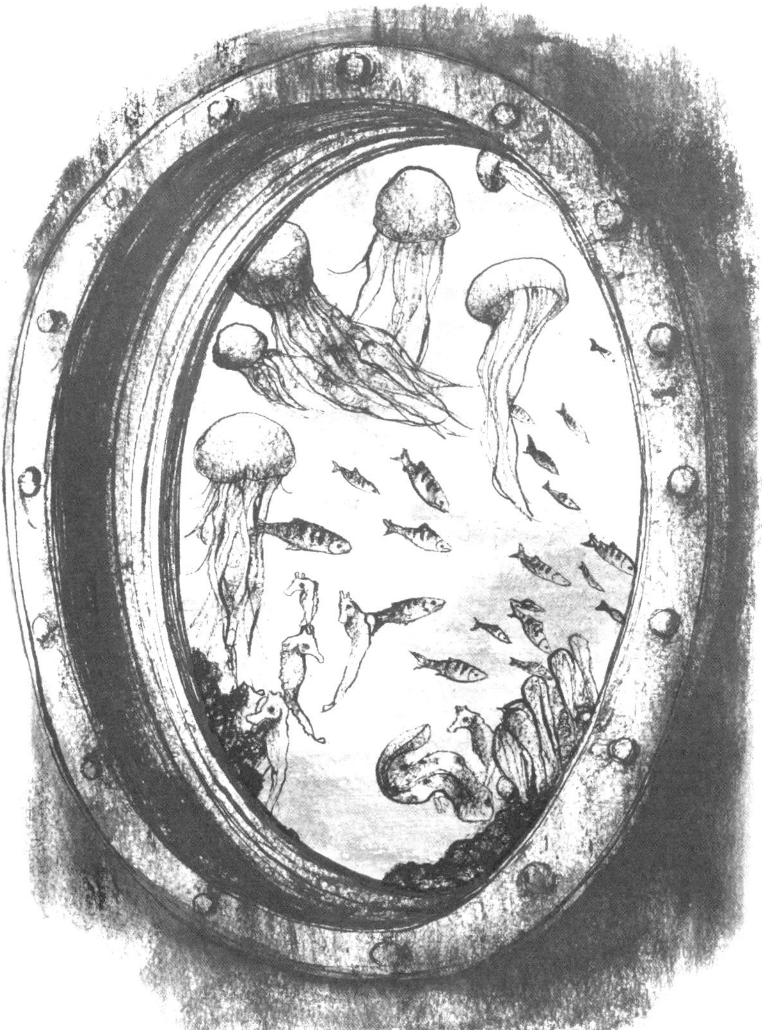

There were mackerel with blue bodies and silvery heads, Japanese salamanders, jellyfish with violet spots, and serpents with sharp teeth. It was like looking into a giant fish tank.

'Well, now we can see what we want, Ned,' I said.

'Yes, I can see that they're free and we're not,' Ned said sourly, pointing at all the fish.

I said nothing. I didn't want to admit it, but I admired Nemo. There was something in his steely determination that made me want to trust him. He loved the sea as I did. And I was happy to be a prisoner if I could learn more than any other scientist in the whole world.

CHAPTER 4

Blood in the water

We sailed for days across the Pacific Ocean. We passed the Galapagos Islands,* where Charles Darwin* had done research for his famous book, *The Origin of Species.*

Giant tortoises, big enough to carry a man on their backs, swam past the window in Nemo's saloon. I watched them with joy, delighted to be following Darwin's trail.

Conseil was happy organising my notes, but Ned was restless. He paced up and down like a caged animal. He was a man of action, not books. Even the sight of the giant tortoises didn't interest him for long. I worried that he might do something to upset Nemo and spoil my chance of studying this beautiful underwater world.

We carried on sailing west along the Equator. Then we headed north until we were 150 miles off the shores of Japan.

Ned's mood improved when we spotted a small group of sperm whales. 'Ah!' he sighed. 'How beautiful they are! It really lifts me up to see them.'

'And yet you make your living killing them,' Captain Nemo said, joining us on deck.

'They give us meat and oil,' Ned replied. 'We need meat and oil to live.'

'Are you sure you only kill for need and not for profit?' Nemo said.

'Talking of reasons for doing things,' Ned said. 'What's your reason for hunting down and sinking ships?'

Nemo looked angry but he didn't answer Ned's question.

'Whales have enough trouble surviving without you hunting them, Ned Land,' Nemo continued. 'Take this school of whales, for example. It's a group of females with their young. And there on the horizon is a pod of orcas* – killer whales – circling for the attack. They will eat the young sperm whales if they can get at them.'

'Then I'll take a harpoon to the orcas,' Ned said. 'Let me save the baby whales, Captain.'

'There's no need for you to risk your life,' Nemo said. 'The *Nautilus* will see them off. Its steel spur is more accurate than your harpoon.'

'The *Nautilus* against the orcas? But that'll be a massacre!' Ned cried.

'What difference does it make if I kill them or you do?' Nemo said.

'They'd have a fair chance against my harpoon,' Ned said.

'This is not a game, Ned Land. It's a matter of life and death,' said Nemo shortly.

The *Nautilus* dived under water. Conseil, Ned and I went below to the window in the saloon, and Captain Nemo took the controls of the *Nautilus*. I soon felt the engines beating faster as we increased our speed.

The female sperm whales swam in a circle with their calves in the middle. They beat their tails to keep the orcas away.

The *Nautilus* moved through the water like a giant harpoon. It hurled itself against the orcas, cutting through them with its deadly spur.

The massacre went on for an hour. There was no escape for the orcas. Several times they tried to crush the *Nautilus*. From the window, we could see their large mouths studded with teeth. We could feel them clinging to the *Nautilus* like a pack of wild dogs.

After a while, the waves became quiet and we rose to the surface. The panel opened, and we hurried onto the deck. The sea was covered with dead whales.

'Well, Master Land?' Nemo said to Ned.

'I am a hunter,' said Ned coldly. 'Not a butcher. And what you've done is butchery.'

'I saved the young whales,' replied the captain. 'Orcas show no mercy and they received none.'

'The orcas wouldn't have killed all the calves,' Ned said. 'They would have just taken what they needed to eat. But you didn't leave one orca alive. You went too far.'

A dead sperm whale rose to the surface of the water in front of us. It lay on its side, full of holes from the bites of the attacking orcas. A dead calf hung from its mother's fin.

The sea lapped quietly over the two dead creatures.

Nemo's action had been cruel but there was some sense in it. He was protecting the calves. But Ned only saw the butchery.

Conseil usually agreed with me, but this time he looked unsure what to think. 'Was Nemo helping nature or did he commit a crime against it?' he asked.

I am not sure why I defended Nemo, but I did. 'Nemo is a brilliant man, and like a lot of brilliant men, he is misunderstood,' I said.

'And like a lot of brilliant men, he's also crazy and dangerous,' Ned argued.

'Perhaps you're both right,' said Conseil wisely. 'But until we know exactly what he means to do, I think we should be careful.'

Ned and I scowled at each other and said nothing.

CHAPTER 5

Birds of paradise

We did not speak to each other for a long time after our argument over the orcas. Ned and I both thought we were right, and Conseil didn't say anything because he didn't want to take sides. Why was I being so stubborn? Was my work more important to me than my friends?

The *Nautilus* sailed south past the Philippines and through the islands of Indonesia until it reached the dangerous shores of the Coral Sea, on the northeast coast of Australia. We passed the reef where Captain Cook the explorer had lost his ship on 11th June 1770.

Shoals of brightly coloured fish swam alongside the *Nautilus*. There were giltheads, dories* and flying fish. The flying fish were like submarine swallows, diving in and out of the waves, and on dark nights they lit up the air and water with their glowing scales.

Two days after crossing the Coral Sea, we spotted the coast of Papua New Guinea. Nemo planned to get into the Indian Ocean through the Straits of Torres.*

The Straits of Torres were full of islands and rocks and it was almost impossible to make our way safely through them.

'This is a bad sea,' Ned said to Nemo, as the *Nautilus* plunged through the waves.

Suddenly the *Nautilus* shuddered and came to a halt, leaning to one side. We had run aground.

'Are we stranded?' I asked Nemo anxiously.

'Yes, but only until the tide turns and lifts us off,' Nemo said. 'It's nothing to worry about.'

Ned looked out at a nearby island, spotting a chance to step onto dry land.

'I see you're looking at the Island of Gilboa, Mr Land,' Nemo said. 'Perhaps you'd like to go ashore?'

'That's right. I was thinking of stealing your

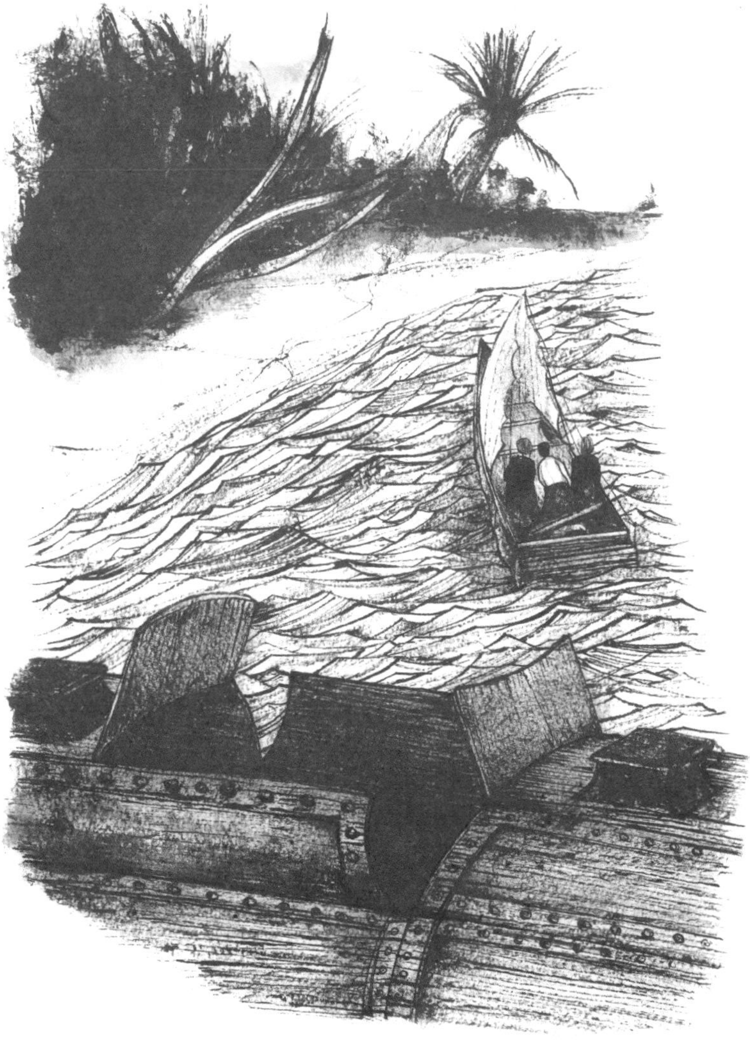

small boat and sailing away,' Ned joked.

'No need to steal it,' Nemo said. 'You're free to use it if you wish. Why don't the three of you go and explore? The tide won't turn for another twelve hours. The *Nautilus* can't sail until then.'

We all looked at Nemo with surprise.

'It's not the mainland,' Nemo explained. 'So you can't run away anywhere.'

We didn't argue and happily borrowed the small boat to sail ashore. It was a great chance for me to make more scientific notes and for Ned to get away from our steel prison. But best of all, it was a great chance for us to make friends again. The three of us chatted excitedly on the small boat as though we had never fallen out.

The island was covered in enormous trees, many tens of metres tall, mingled with swaying palms, white orchids and green ferns.

'If the island has plenty of food and fresh water, I vote we stay here until another ship passes by and rescues us,' Ned said.

'But what if Nemo and his men follow us ashore?' Conseil said.

'Stop it!' I said. 'This island is full of plants

and animals that I haven't seen before. I'm going to record my findings before I do anything else.'

'Fine, Professor,' Ned said. 'We'll see what the island has to offer first before we make any plans.'

Ned and Conseil looked for food while I looked for wildlife. They collected fruit and coconuts. Ned split open a coconut and we drank the milk. It was sweet and cool and delicious, and Ned promised to make a pie out of the fruit. We were all glad to have a change from seafood after a couple of months on board the *Nautilus*.

I saw kingfishers, parrots and cockatoos of all colours. And in a clearing, I saw several birds with long, brilliantly coloured feathers, swooping around in graceful circles.

'Birds of paradise,' I cried. 'And so beautiful!'

A herd of kangaroos sprang out of the bushes and Ned hopped along with them, holding his hands to his chest like kangaroo paws. Conseil and I laughed so much we scared the birds away.

As the sun went down, we built a fire and

Ned made the fruit pie he had promised us. It was delicious. We sat back and relaxed in the firelight.

'So, Professor,' Ned said. 'What do you think now? Should we take our chances and stay?'

'It's large enough to find a hiding place,' Conseil said. 'Nemo would never find us.'

I felt a sharp pain of misery. I wanted to go back to the *Nautilus*. But I didn't know how to tell my friends. There were so many more things I wanted to see that only the *Nautilus* could show me. Ned and Conseil were looking at me with hope in their eyes. How could I ask them to give up their chance of escape just so that I could find out more about the science of the oceans?

But before I could give them an answer, a stone flew through the air and hit our fire, spraying sparks everywhere.

'Stones don't just fall from the sky,' Conseil said.

He was right. Someone had thrown the stone. Suddenly, the faces of several Papuan men were lit up by the fire's glow. They threw more stones at us and shouted angrily. We were uninvited guests in their home and they were not going to let us stay.

'Quick!' I yelled. 'Back to the boat.' We leaped to our feet and ran. The Papuans chased us. They were armed with bows and arrows, and wore nets around their necks full of stones, which they threw at us.

We reached the boat and shoved off, splashing into the waves. The Papuans yelled with rage and followed us into the water.

Scrambling on board, we grabbed the oars and rowed for our lives. The Papuans ran along the shore to their canoes. Moments later they were paddling after us. Their canoes, made of tree trunks, were long and narrow and they were much faster than our little boat.

'Put up the sail,' Conseil panted.

'There's no wind,' Ned said. 'It's row or die.'

We put our backs into it, pulling for all we were worth. I thought the canoes would reach us before we made the safety of the *Nautilus*, but Ned kept shouting for us to row faster. Just as we came alongside the *Nautilus*, the Papuans fired their arrows. They swished past our heads and pinged off the steel sides of the *Nautilus*.

Ned fixed the small boat to the *Nautilus* and we dived headlong down the open hatch, landing in a heap at the foot of the ladder. I staggered to my feet, stumbled along the corridor and burst breathlessly into the saloon.

Nemo was at the piano. My crashing entrance* did not surprise him and he didn't stop playing.

'Nemo, we're under attack. The islanders are attacking us,' I stammered.

'Relax, Professor. Arrows are no match for the *Nautilus*.'

'But they're going to climb on board!'

Nemo casually pressed an electric button on a panel next to the piano and went on playing. What did the button do? How could Nemo stay so calm?

I turned and raced back to the hatch expecting to fight hand-to-hand with the islanders. Ned and Conseil were at the bottom of the ladder, fists clenched and ready for action.

A tremor shook the *Nautilus*. I heard its keel* grating against the coral beneath.

'The tide is turning,' Ned said. 'The *Nautilus* is floating free.'

At that moment a head appeared at the opening of the hatch. The islander jabbed at us with a spear but he couldn't reach. He put his hand on the ladder and then let out a terrifying yell. His head jerked backwards and disappeared. A second later another head came into view. A hand came out and gripped the ladder, and another terrifying scream split the night.

'What's going on?' Ned asked. He put his hand on the ladder as the islanders had done – and was immediately thrown backwards.

He landed with a jolt and lay there groaning.

'I put an electric current through the ladder,' Nemo said, coming up behind us. 'The button I pressed in the saloon switched it on. It won't kill, but it will hurt enough to keep anyone out.'

'And keep prisoners in,' Ned moaned, shaking his tingling hand.

'You weren't thinking of leaving, were you, Mr Land?' Nemo said.

Conseil helped Ned to his feet.

'I hope you had a good trip to the island, Professor,' Nemo said, smiling.

I wanted to thank Nemo, but I knew it would make Ned and Conseil angry, so I just nodded.

The *Nautilus* stirred and was finally free of the coral reef. I sighed with relief. I was also free. Free from having to make up my mind about joining my friends in their bid to escape. I had been saved in more ways than one.

CHAPTER 6

Shark attack

Ned sank into another deep silence, angry that we had not managed to stay on the island and find a rescue ship. Conseil helped me with my notes, but he only did it to keep his mind off being a prisoner. I, however, was glad to be aboard the *Nautilus*. I was sure there were more amazing scientific discoveries ahead of us.

As we passed by the Island of Ceylon in the northern part of the Indian Ocean, Captain Nemo invited us to take a walk underwater to visit the pearl fisheries.

'Impossible,' Ned said when he got the invitation. 'No one can walk underwater.'

It was surprising enough to live in a submarine,

but to discover it was also possible to breathe underwater in a suit left us all in shock.

Nemo showed us the amazing diving suits on board the *Nautilus*. A metal tank of pressurised air was strapped to our backs. Two rubber hoses came out at the top and were attached to a mouthpiece. A copper helmet was placed over our heads.

'I feel like a sardine in a tin,' Ned said from inside his helmet.

'Well, let's hope nothing on the seabed fancies a sardine,' Conseil joked.

'I can't wait to walk under the water,' I said. 'At last I'll be close enough to see and touch what I'm trying to research.'

'You are not afraid of sharks, then?' Nemo said, smiling faintly.

'Sharks!' I repeated, gulping nervously.

'Don't worry,' he said. 'We'll be armed.'

I broke out in a sweat while the captain went off to get the small boat ready for the dive.

Ned was excited at leaving the prison of the *Nautilus* again, if only for a short while.

Conseil was less sure. 'Research is starting to become a daft excuse for accepting invitations from a madman,' he said.

'I agree,' Ned said. 'But if we leave the *Nautilus*, we can explore the chances of escape. If we're near the coast, maybe we could walk to freedom.'

'But what about the sharks?' I said. I was angry that Ned was still thinking about escape, and I wanted to frighten him.

'Sharks don't scare me, if I've got a good harpoon,' Ned said calmly.

Nothing scared Ned Land. He would fight a shark for the fun of it, but I was terrified of even being in the water with one.

Conseil had once said that I would give up my freedom for science. I now realised that even though I was afraid, I would also give up my life for it. In the past, people had carried on with scientific research – even when their lives were at risk. And they had changed the world for the better. Helping others through science *was* worth dying for.

'Well, what about you, Conseil?' I said. 'Are you ready to risk being eaten by a shark?'

'I'm learning that while life is definitely safer behind a desk, it's not so exciting,' Conseil said. 'Besides, we're a team, aren't we? Where one goes, we all go.'

Ned and I slapped Conseil on the back. The three of us were very different, but he was right. We were still friends.

We finished putting on our diving suits, and

left the *Nautilus* in the small boat. Once we were out in the middle of the bay, Ned jumped into the water carrying his harpoon. Nemo gave me and Conseil a small dagger each. We looked at these daggers in panic. They didn't look big enough to fight a goldfish, never mind a shark. But we followed him into the water.

The sun's rays reached down to the bottom of the seabed, reflecting off the backs of silver fish. Every rock, flower, shell and fish shone like a rainbow. It was more beautiful than I can describe.

Walking along the seabed, Captain Nemo pointed to the clusters of oysters attached to the rocks.

I loved being in the water, even though there was the chance of becoming a shark's dinner. Fish swam before me like sparkling jewels. Plant life swayed in the gentle currents. I knew I was seeing things that no other scientist had ever seen.

A shadow fell across me. I ducked, scared that it might be a shark. But I was wrong. It was a man – an Indian fisherman. I could see

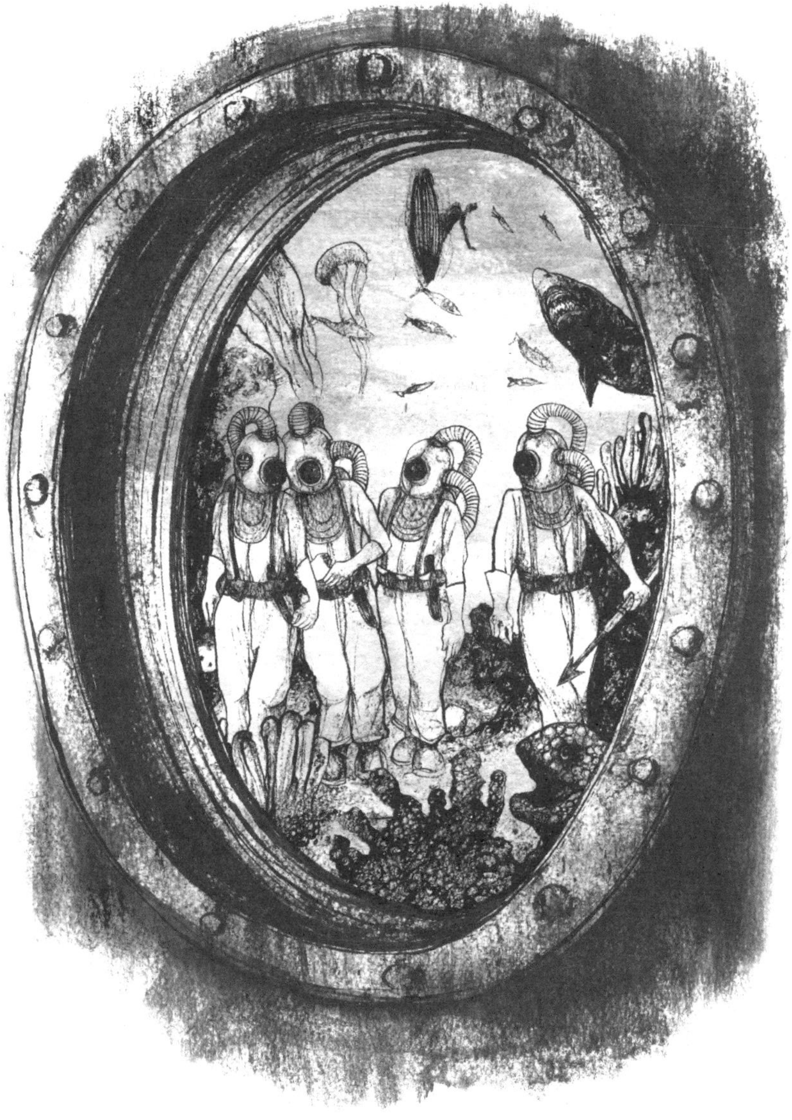

the bottom of his canoe above our heads on the surface of the water. He dived again and again, filling a bag with oysters each time. We were hidden behind a rock so the diver didn't notice us.

As we watched, the diver turned and suddenly looked terrified. He leaped for the safety of his canoe.

A huge shark was swimming towards him, its eyes on fire and its jaws open. The diver flung himself to one side and the shark missed its prey. But its tail thrashed and knocked the poor man to the seabed. I was speechless with horror and unable to move.

The shark circled, getting ready for a second attack.

Captain Nemo took out his dagger and walked straight towards the monster, ready to fight face to face.

The shark's jaws opened wide, showing rows of razor-sharp teeth, and with a flick of its tail it fired itself forward like a bullet.

Nemo swerved at the last minute and buried his dagger deep into the shark's side. Through swirling red waters I saw Nemo hanging on to one of the creature's fins, but he fell back as the shark shook him off. Its jaws snapped greedily together as it got ready to dive in for the kill.

I wanted to help the captain and grabbed my knife, but my fingers were like jelly and I couldn't get the knife out of my belt. But Ned, his harpoon in his hand, rushed towards the shark and struck it a deadly blow. After a few seconds it went limp and lifeless.

Ned helped the captain to his feet. Then Nemo went to the diver, took him in his arms and swam to the surface. The diver opened his eyes and stared in fear as Nemo laid him in his canoe.

'He'll live,' Nemo said calmly. Then he gave Ned a cold smile.

'Thank you, Master Land,' he said, 'for saving my life.'

'You saved me from drowning. Now we're even,' Ned replied. 'I don't owe you anything any more.'

All this took only a few minutes, but it taught me a lot. I now knew that Nemo was a man of great courage. He wouldn't think twice about risking his life. He was ready to die for a man he didn't even know. But it gave me no more clues about his history. Why had he decided to live outside the law? Why did he hate the outside world so much?

'I should have let him end up in the jaws of a shark,' Ned said later. 'Then his crew would have let us go.'

'No, they wouldn't,' I said angrily. 'They

would have blamed us for his death and killed us for sure.'

'You saved him because you're not ruled by hatred, Ned,' Conseil said. 'You should be glad that you're not like Nemo. He's letting his hatred of the world destroy him.'

'But Nemo saved the diver,' I told them. 'So he can't be as bad as you two think.'

But what did I *really think?* Was I under his spell? Or did I just want to know all the secrets of the sea that Nemo promised to show me? Why had he attacked our ship? Maybe he was a murderer, or was he a victim of terrible injustice?*

CHAPTER 7

Trapped

The *Nautilus* sailed from the Indian Ocean into the Southern Ocean and our underwater landscape changed quickly. Icebergs drifted by the window, shining ghostly white. Was Nemo mad enough to be heading for the South Pole? Many ships had sunk attempting to reach the pole.

For several weeks my friends and I had argued about Nemo.

'But one thing is sure,' I said. 'Nemo is an amazing man. And he knows more about the sea than anyone in the world.'

'He's clever, all right,' Ned agreed. 'But he's also as cold as the icebergs we're sailing past.'

The following morning at three o'clock, the *Nautilus* rocked violently and I was thrown from my bed.

'Have we had an accident?' I asked Nemo.

'Yes,' he answered shortly. 'An iceberg has turned over and fallen on us.'

'Has it done any damage?' I asked.

'It has trapped us,' Nemo said. 'It struck the *Nautilus* as it fell, and then it floated back up and pinned us under a sheet of ice.'

Ned and Conseil, also shaken from their beds, joined us in the saloon.

'We are floating in a box of ice,' Nemo said.

We could see the four ice walls through the observation window. The electric light from the *Nautilus* made the white surfaces dazzlingly bright.

'Gentlemen,' Nemo said calmly. 'We face two ways of dying. One, we may be crushed by the ice. Or two, we may suffocate. We only have forty-eight hours of air left in the tanks.'

'Can we escape within forty-eight hours?' I asked.

'We are going to try and break through the thinnest wall of ice which lies below us,' Nemo said.

Ten metres of ice separated the *Nautilus* from clear water below. Nemo calculated that we needed to dig out 600 cubic metres to make a hole large enough for the *Nautilus* to get through.

The crew set to work straight away. Wearing specially padded diving suits, they drilled into the ice and then attacked it with their pickaxes. Chips of ice floated off into the water as the crew worked. All of us took a turn in the water with a pickaxe. Our lives depended on it.

We worked two-hour shifts at a time. When I came back to the *Nautilus* I noticed a difference between the pure air of the diving tanks and the poor air in the *Nautilus*. On board, we were slowly being poisoned.

After twelve hours we had only dug out one metre of ice. At that rate, it would take five nights and four days to break out, but we only had enough air for two more days.

On my next shift I noticed that the three walls we were not digging into seemed to be getting nearer. The ice was closing in on the *Nautilus*! The three walls were growing thicker and would soon crush the submarine like glass.

'Our only chance is to dig quicker than the walls freeze up,' Nemo said.

Soon, the air aboard the *Nautilus* became so bad that we all looked forward to going out to work and breathing the pure air of our diving tanks.

That evening the trench was one metre deeper, but the sidewalls of the ice box had also grown a lot thicker. We weren't going to make it before the ice closed in.

Nemo paced the saloon. 'We must stop the other walls from freezing up,' he said. Then an idea struck him. 'Boiling water!' he muttered.

'Boiling water?' I cried.

'Yes, Professor. Jets of boiling water fired

at the walls will stop them from freezing so quickly.'

'Of course,' I agreed.

During the night the *Nautilus* pumped out boiling water into the sea around us. The temperature rose enough to stop the walls of ice closing in any further.

Six metres of ice had been cleared by morning. Only four metres were left. But we only had one more day of air left.

Towards the end of the day my lungs panted as they struggled for oxygen. The air aboard the *Nautilus* was almost finished and there were still two metres of ice to break through. The air that was left was kept for the workers. Not a breath of it was pumped into the *Nautilus*. When I returned from my shift I gasped for breath and my head was dizzy with pain.

Captain Nemo knew that we would never make it in time. We could not work fast enough with the pickaxes. There was only one small, last chance. Nemo decided to try and ram the *Nautilus* through the rest of the layer of ice.

His face stern, Nemo revved the engines and

dived to the bottom of the trench at full speed. We hit the ice where we had been digging like a sledgehammer. There was a terrible cracking, tearing sound and the *Nautilus* shuddered like a live creature – and floated free!

'We're going to do it!' Conseil cried in delight.

But I lay suffocating slowly. My face was purple and my lips turned blue. I could not think. I drifted for a few moments and then everything went black.

A rush of air revived me. Had we risen to the surface already? No, it was Ned and Conseil. A scrap of air was left in one of the diving tanks. Instead of using it for themselves, they had kept it for me. While they were being suffocated, they gave me life, drop by drop.

I tried to push the tank away but I was too weak, and for some moments I breathed freely.

Seconds later, the diving instruments of the *Nautilus* told us we were ten metres from the surface. Only a thin crust of ice separated us from the open air.

Again the *Nautilus* attacked the ice sheet like a huge battering ram, only this time from beneath. There was a shattering, crunching sound, as it broke through, shooting forwards and upwards and then crushing the ice beneath it as it landed. Oxygen flowed into everyone's lungs. We were saved! Everybody aboard cheered with their first gulps of fresh, pure air.

We had worked together as a team, and I felt more a part of the *Nautilus* crew than ever.

'But if it wasn't for Nemo, we wouldn't have been trapped in the first place,' Ned argued. 'When will you see sense, Professor? What good will your science do you when you're dead?'

The sensible part of me agreed with Ned. At first, Nemo had seemed calm and in control, but now he was behaving more and more strangely.

Time and time again, he was putting us in danger.

But another part of me didn't want to agree with Ned. I wanted to follow Nemo, and I wanted to make the scientific discoveries that only he could show me.

CHAPTER 8

Freak of nature

Nemo set off at full speed towards the north and we found ourselves in the Atlantic Ocean off the South Americas.

Ned sat by the chest of Spanish doubloons.* He loved looking into their golden glow. It was one of the few pleasures he had aboard the *Nautilus*, but he never took even one coin. Ned Land was as honest as he was brave. But Nemo would not have cared if Ned had taken any; he said there was plenty more gold in the sea where that had come from.

Conseil had covered the desk with maps of the world, trying to work out where the *Nautilus* was heading.

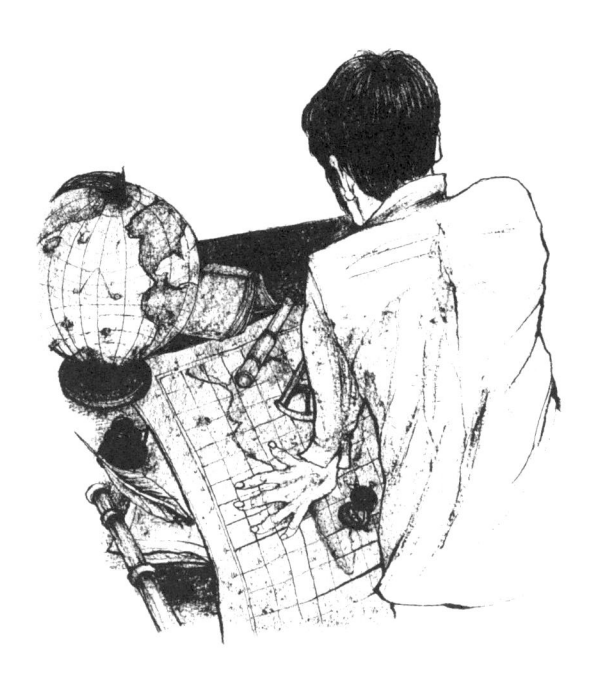

Was Nemo sailing the seas without a plan, or was he searching for something or someone? He seemed to want revenge.

I was now used to the wonders I saw every day and I didn't think there was anything left in the sea to shock me. But I was wrong. The oceans had a terrible surprise in store for us.

I was making notes on what I saw through the window when a fantastic monster swam before my eyes. It was a giant squid, close to eight metres long. It swam with the *Nautilus*, staring in through the window with bright green eyes. Its tentacles lashed furiously and its mouth was like a parrot's beak, snapping open and shut. A horny tongue and several rows of pointed teeth darted in and out of the beak. It was a bird's beak on a sea creature.

What a freak of nature!

My hand was shaking, but I picked up a pencil and began to draw the monster for my records.

As I drew, several more swam up to the window and gnashed their beaks against the glass. A sudden shock went through the *Nautilus* and brought it to a sharp stop.

As I looked up from my drawing, Captain Nemo came into the saloon.

'They're a scary bunch,' I said, nodding at the creatures.

'Yes, they are, Mr Naturalist,' he replied. 'And we've got to get out there and fight them.'

'Out there?' Conseil repeated, alarmed. 'What a nightmare! What's happened?'

'Our propeller has stopped. The horny jaws of that first squid are caught in it,' Nemo explained. 'We've got to get the *Nautilus* to the surface and take them out with hatchets.'*

'And a harpoon,' Ned said. 'No giant squid is going to get Ned Land without a fight.'

'I'll help,' Conseil said. He turned to me and whispered under his breath. 'On deck I might see a landmark to help me work out where we are.'

I said I would help too. I was learning to conquer my fears and had grown used to facing danger with my friends.

We followed the captain to the main stairs where ten of the crew were ready with hatchets. Ned grabbed a harpoon. Conseil and I took a hatchet each. The *Nautilus* rose to the surface and one of the sailors unscrewed the bolts of the main hatch. But before he could open it fully, the cover was ripped from his hands by a giant tentacle.

Another tentacle slid down the opening like a serpent, and there were at least another twenty waving about above. With one blow of his axe, Captain Nemo cut the first tentacle off and it slithered down the ladder.

As we all pushed forward to reach the deck, another tentacle snatched at the leading sailor. It tore him from the ladder and dragged him out of the *Nautilus*. Captain Nemo rushed out and we hurried after him.

The sailor danced in the air at the end of the tentacle. He screamed in fear. Captain Nemo ran at the squid and cut off another tentacle. Several other monsters crept up the sides of the *Nautilus*. The crew swung their axes in rage and desperation. Ned, Conseil and I joined in, hacking wildly.

The first squid had only one tentacle left, waving the sailor in the air like a feather. But just as Captain Nemo ran forward again, the monster squirted a stream of black liquid* and blinded us all. When the black cloud cleared away, the giant squid had gone, taking the sailor with it.

Then ten more monstrous creatures charged at the *Nautilus*. Mad with horror and rage, we hacked into the mass of slimy tentacles. Ned struck his harpoon into the staring eyes of a giant squid. But a tentacle whipped around his feet and knocked him down. I rushed to help him, but Captain Nemo was faster. He thrust his axe between the squid's enormous jaws, stopping it in its tracks.

'Now you owe me again, Ned Land,' Nemo laughed.

Ned was furious to be once again in Nemo's debt and he grabbed his harpoon. But Nemo laughed even louder, as though he wanted Ned to run him through. White-faced, Ned controlled his anger and turned his harpoon back on the squid.

After quarter of an hour's desperate fighting, the monsters slipped down under the waves.

Captain Nemo, exhausted and covered with blood, stared out at the sea that had swallowed up one of his friends. Tears came into his eyes. He would not speak to any of us and went below to his cabin. There he stayed for several days.

The *Nautilus* drifted, waiting for orders from its captain, floating on the waves like a dead body.

CHAPTER 9

Last battle

As the *Nautilus* drifted, I carried on with my work. During our months at sea, I had made enough notes to write another book. I wondered if Nemo would let me publish it. My thoughts about the book were interrupted when Ned burst into the saloon.

'Professor, Nemo is feeling sorry for his dead friend and we must try and make him feel sorry for us too. We must beg him to let us go. Surely even he has seen too much blood to want to kill us now.'

I agreed to talk to Nemo. Ned was going crazy cooped up in the *Nautilus*. And even though I was still not ready to leave, I knew that Ned would do something desperate if he had to stay locked up for much longer. Surely Nemo could see that and he would let my friends go?

But Nemo would not listen to me.

'No one is allowed to leave the *Nautilus*,' he said calmly. 'Ever.'

I told Ned and Conseil what Nemo had said. There was no use hiding the truth from them.

'Well, at least we know where we are,' Ned said. 'Conseil has worked it out. The *Nautilus* is drifting past the coast of New York. If we try tonight, there's a chance of reaching land.'

I didn't say anything, but prayed for bad weather to change their plans. Nemo seemed to be mad, but I could not hate him. I wanted to help him and still save my friends.

That night, as though my prayers had been answered, a storm blew up and swept the *Nautilus* far out to sea. Any hope of escaping to the shores of New York faded away.

Some days later, the *Nautilus* stopped drifting and began to sail in large circles as though it was looking for something. Captain Nemo came out of his cabin. He did not speak a word to me, and looked so pale and desperate that I felt afraid. Was there some new disaster? Was he planning something terrible? Were we about to discover the truth about his past?

A dull boom rocked the *Nautilus*, but Nemo showed no signs of surprise.

We went on deck and found Ned and Conseil already looking out to sea.

'It was a gunshot,' Ned explained.

A huge ship was speeding towards the *Nautilus*.

'What ship is that?' I asked Ned.

'It's a battleship, but I can't see what country she's from,' Ned said. Then he leaned towards me and whispered, 'If that ship passes within a mile of us, we can throw ourselves into the sea and swim for it.'

Another large rocket exploded in the water and rocked the *Nautilus*.

Ned whipped out his handkerchief and waved it in the air, but it was struck down by the iron hand of Nemo.

'Fool!' Nemo said quietly. 'How can they save you? In another minute that ship will be lying at the bottom of the sea.'

'Are you – are you going to attack it?' I stammered stupidly.

'Attack it and sink it,' he said.

'You can't do that!' I cried.

'I can and I will,' he said coldly. 'Now the three of you must go down below.'

'But what ship is it?' I asked.

'You don't know?' Nemo said. 'Good. It's better that you don't. Now go below.'

There was nothing we could do but obey.

Nemo shouted at the ship as it came closer. 'Fire away, you fools! You will not escape the *Nautilus*. I am the law, and I am the judge. I have lost all that I loved – country, wife, children, father and mother. I shall have my revenge.'

'That's not all he's lost,' Conseil muttered to me. 'He's lost his mind.'

The *Nautilus* powered towards the battleship, aiming to ram it. The two ships crashed into one another, and I fell to my feet with the shock of impact. The steel spur of the *Nautilus* tore through the battleship's hull, screeching against the steel as it went.

Through the window I saw the ship sinking before me. Water rushed through it with the noise of thunder. Sailors ran in every direction. It looked like a human ant heap flooded by the sea. I stood and watched, frozen with horror and unable to help in any way.

Captain Nemo joined us in the saloon to watch the ship slip beneath the waves. When the ship had disappeared into the dark depths below, Nemo walked quietly to his cabin. On the end wall of his room, I saw the portrait of a young woman and two young children. Captain

Nemo looked at them, stretched his arms towards them and cried.

 I knew then that the wounds of his past were too deep to heal. And they were too private for him to ever talk about to a prisoner like me. I would never know what lay at the heart of this man.

PART 3

CHAPTER 10

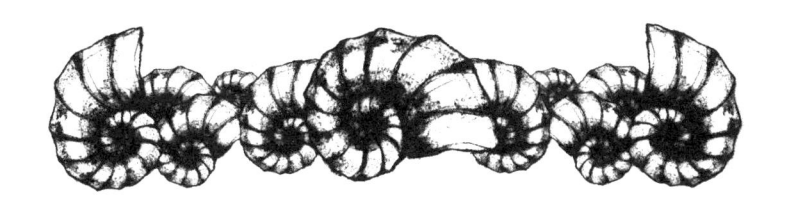

Maelstrom

I went to my room but I slept badly. The horrible sight of the sinking battleship kept coming into my head. I hadn't thought it would ever happen, but I now hated the sea. It was a place of great beauty but it was also a cruel killer, and I knew if I stayed much longer I would be its next victim.

I awoke from another nightmare to see Ned and Conseil standing over me.

'Professor,' Ned said. 'Tonight's the night. We are going to escape at last.'

'But where are we?' I cried, still half-asleep.

'In sight of land. It's twenty miles to the east,' Ned answered.

'And what country is it?'

'We don't know,' Conseil admitted. 'But whatever it is, that's where we are going.'

I sat up and saw that Ned and Conseil meant business. I thought again of the dead sailors being dragged down inside their doomed battleship.

'You're right,' I said. 'It's time to go. I would die for science, but I will not let others die for me.'

'And I will die for my freedom,' Ned said quietly. 'If anybody tries to stop me, I will fight them to the death.'

'I understand,' I said. 'Let's meet in half an hour on board the small boat.'

The others went back to their cabins to get their things. I put on my strong sea clothes, then collected all my research notes and put them in a leather wallet. My heart thumped in my chest, as I got ready to leave.

At that moment I heard the piano in the saloon. Nemo was playing a sad tune. It sounded like a cry of pain.

I had to creep past Nemo to reach the door

that led to the small boat. The saloon was in darkness, but I hoped that he wouldn't hear me above the sounds of the piano. Even if there had been a light on, I don't think Nemo would have noticed me. He was too lost in his music.

I reached the door and was just about to open it when the music stopped. A sigh from Captain Nemo froze me to the spot. I heard him rising from his seat. Then I caught a glimpse of him as he walked into the light that shone into the saloon from his cabin. He came towards me silently, with his arms crossed, gliding like a ghost. His breathing sounded shallow and his voice broke as he said the last words I ever heard from him. 'Enough! Enough!'

Had he had enough of his revenge? Was his conscience getting the better of him?

I rushed out of the door without looking back, not knowing if Nemo had seen me or not. I leaped up the ladder that led to the small boat and crept through the opening. Ned and Conseil were already aboard.

'Let's go,' I said quickly.

Ned closed the manhole cover behind us. Then he tried loosening the bolts that fixed the small boat to the *Nautilus* with a gadget he had made himself.

Loud voices from inside the *Nautilus* made Ned pause. What was the matter? Had they discovered we were missing? I felt Ned slip a dagger into my hand.

'So,' I murmured. 'This is how we shall die.'

We sat and waited, daggers in hand and ready to fight, but no one came. All we heard was one word from inside the *Nautilus* repeated over and over again by the sailors… 'Maelstrom!'* they kept saying.

The maelstrom is a violent whirlpool off the coast of Norway, which few ships have ever escaped from. The *Nautilus* was caught in its swirling grip. Had Nemo steered towards it on purpose? Did he want to die?

'Quickly,' I said to Ned. 'Undo the bolts. We must get free before the whirlpool takes too strong a hold of the *Nautilus*.' But Ned was already struggling with the bolts.

'It's no use,' he said. 'The gadget I made doesn't fit. It won't turn them.'

'Then we're trapped,' Conseil said. 'And we'll drown with Nemo.'

We sat in silence for a moment, thinking that we were going to die. The sound of the raging waters outside grew louder, and the boat rocked more and more violently. The steel plates of the *Nautilus* creaked under the strain.

'We must hold on,' Ned said. 'Maybe the *Nautilus* will get free.'

He had hardly finished speaking when we heard the bolts groan and saw them turn

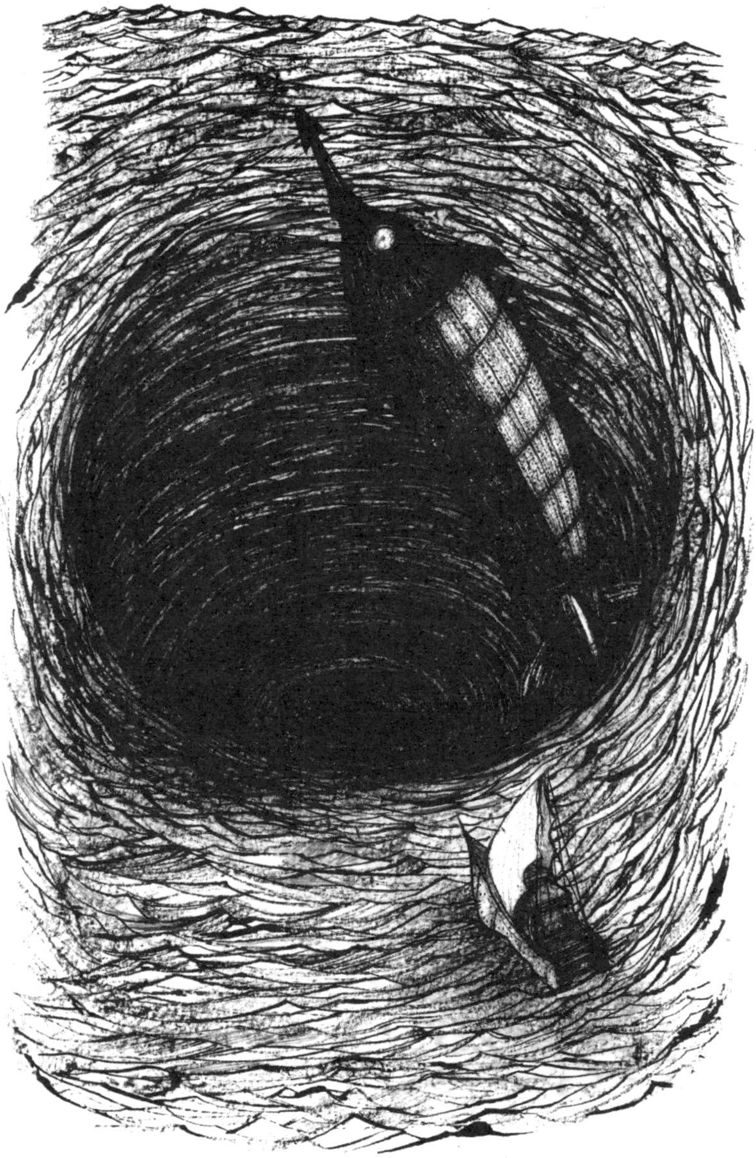

without the help of Ned's home-made key. Was it the violence of the water that was freeing us, or an unseen hand from inside the *Nautilus*? Was this Nemo's last good act? The bolts gave way, and the boat was hurled like a stone towards the edge of the whirlpool.

Then my head struck against the steel side of the boat, and everything went jumbled and dark.

CHAPTER 11

Final words

When I came round, I was lying in a fisherman's hut on the Lofoden Isles.* Ned and Conseil were safe and sound, sitting next to me. They grinned from ear to ear when they saw me wake up. Conseil held up my leather wallet full of notes. He'd saved them for me. I grinned back at my friends.

We had been set free from the *Nautilus* just in time. Ned and Conseil had raised the mast of our small boat and sailed away from the maelstrom until our boat had capsized in the heavy seas. Stranded on the upturned boat, we had then been rescued by Norwegian fishermen.

But what happened to the *Nautilus*?

Did it escape the pull of the maelstrom? Is Captain Nemo still alive? Does he slip from ocean to ocean, still sinking ships? And will I ever learn who he really was?

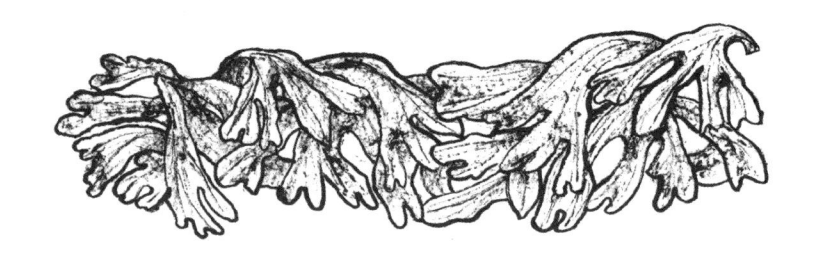

If he lives, then I can only hope that his hatred softens. Perhaps the wonders on show below the waves will one day cool his desire for revenge and he will explore the seas in peace.

I have told my story as honestly as I can remember it. I am not proud to remember some of what I did. But everything I've written is the truth. Will anyone believe me? Will my research be worth anything if they don't?

Whatever happens, I shall never forget my journey of 20,000 leagues under the sea.

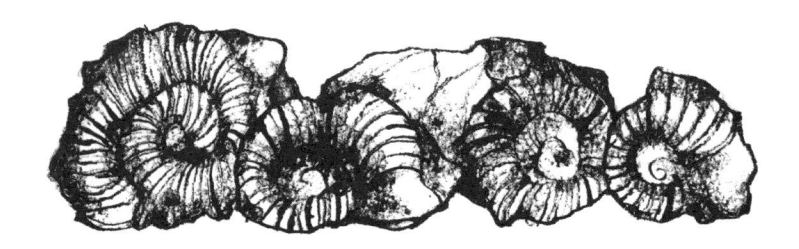

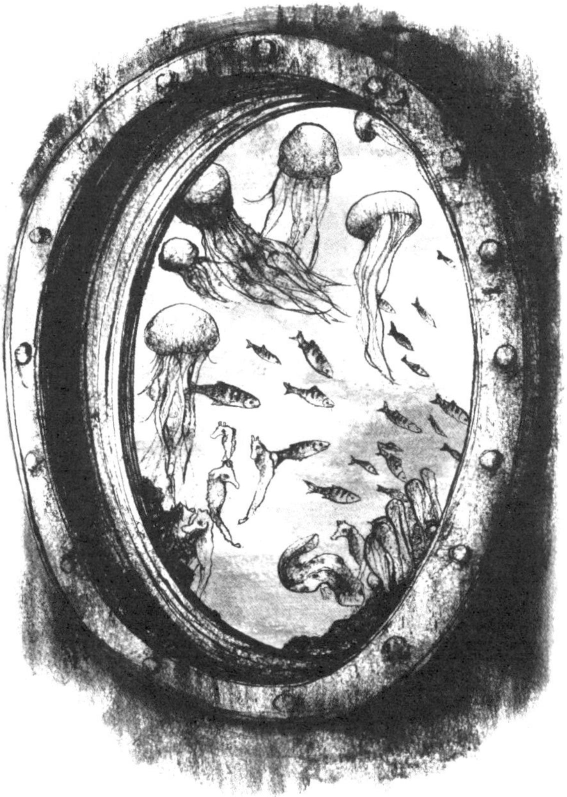

Jules Verne
(born 1828, died 1905)

Jules Gabriel Verne was born in France, in a city called Nantes. Nantes was a busy harbour city, and when he was young, Jules would often row a boat around the harbour with his younger brother, where he found the sight of all the ships very exciting. This stirred his imagination, and he would later write about inventions in his science fiction stories that were uncannily accurate in their predictions of future transportation and technology.

After his schooling, Verne went to Paris to study law but discovered that he preferred to write stories. He worked as a stockbroker to support himself in his early days as a writer. He was fortunate to meet some of France's most famous writers, such as Alexandre Dumas, who offered him advice on writing.

Verne's books were rejected by many publishers. Eventually, he found a publisher who helped him to rewrite his stories to improve them, and he published his first book *Five Weeks in a Balloon* – although Verne knew nothing about ballooning! Jules Verne stayed with this publisher for the rest of his writing career.

Verne became famous and wealthy through his writing, and his books are still among the most translated in the world.

Best known works
Around the World in Eighty Days
Journey to the Centre of the Earth

David Tomlinson

David grew up on the east coast of North Yorkshire, and despite coming close to drowning after capsizing a catamaran (the Coastguard were called out to rescue him), his love of the sea has never diminished. Perhaps that's why he enjoyed working on this book so much.

David read a lot of books as a child and by the age of ten he knew he wanted to be a writer when he left school. He wrote story after story in his spare time until finally selling a script to television at the age of twenty-two.

David became a professional scriptwriter, script editor and television producer and worked for many years at the BBC developing new comic writers and performers. He has worked on BBC shows *Cavegirl* and *Bruiser*.

This is his first adaptation of a book. David says, 'I chose to adapt *20,000 Leagues Under the Sea* because I remembered my own excitement at reading the book when I was a teenager. I wanted to see if I could bring the "Father of Science Fiction", Jules Verne, to the attention of younger readers.'

Notes about this book

Jules Verne wrote about several types of travel before they had actually been invented: space travel, air travel, and travelling underwater. In *20,000 Leagues Under the Sea,* he describes a long voyage in a submarine before technology of this kind existed. The number of leagues in the title refers to the distance they travelled, not the depth that they reached under the sea. Travelling 20,000 leagues is the equivalent of going around the world twice!

It is interesting to note that a teacher at Verne's boarding school in France was an inventor who later designed the first submarine for the US navy. It is from him that Verne may have got the idea for this book.

Page 7
***fossils** The hard remains of animals and plants that lived millions of years ago that have set in rock.
***harpoons** Long steel spears used to kill whales.

Page 10
***algae** Tiny one-cell creatures which together form large areas on the surface of water, for example, pond scum.

Page 13
***waterspouts** Fountains of water rising from the sea.

Page 15
***rudder** The device that is used to steer a ship.

Page 16
*__hull__ The frame of a ship.

Page 17
*__manhole__ A round entrance, just big enough for one person to fit through, usually with a removable iron or steel cover.

Page 20
*__prisoners of war__ People who are captured by the enemy during a battle or war and are kept prisoner until the war has ended.

Page 22
*__lost city of Atlantis__ A mythical city, said to be an island in the Atlantic Ocean, which was covered by the sea thousands of years ago.

Page 23
*__galleons__ Large Spanish warships.

Page 25
*__blowholes__ The holes on top of the body of a whale, through which it breathes.

Page 29
*__Galapagos Islands__ A cluster of islands off the coast of Ecuador, in South America. They are famous for their giant tortoises.
*__Charles Darwin__ The 19th century scientist who provided evidence to explain the evolution of plant and animal life.

Pages 30–31
* **pod of orcas** 'Pod' is the word (collective noun) for a group of whales.

Pages 36–37
* **giltheads, dories** These are types of fish.
* **Straits of Torres** The stretch of sea between northern Australia and Papua New Guinea.

Page 44
* **crashing entrance** To enter the room in a noisy or clumsy way.
* **keel** The bottom of a ship.

Page 56
* **injustice** When something bad happens that is very unfair.

Page 66
* **doubloons** Old Spanish gold coins.

Page 69
* **hatchets** A hatchet is a light axe with a short handle.

Page 71
* **black liquid** A squid squirts out a black liquid, or ink, when it is afraid or under stress.

Page 85
* **maelstrom** A large whirlpool – water moving fast in a spiral pattern, that can draw a ship in and suck it below the surface.

Page 88
* **Lofoden Isles** A group of islands off the coast of Norway.